What Does Super Jonny do When Mum Gets Sick?

U.K. Version
Suitable for ages 3-9 years

Written by Simone Colwill
Illustrated by Jasmine Ting

"This is a wonderful story...' 'Teachers and parents will find this book invaluable..."
- Booksellers New Zealand

"I look forward to sharing this book with teachers and children."
- Prof Early Childhood, Auckland University.

"Auckland mum's book aims to help children with a parent in hospital"
- NZ Doctor Magazine.

Dedications
Simone: *For my wonderful family.*
Jasmine: *For my parents, my sister Jess, and my supportive friends.*

For more copies of this book, tips for moms coping with chronic illness, and to join our community, please visit our website: www.sickmom.org

For Educators (see guide notes on page 32). Suitable for ages 3-9 years* *subject matter.

North America: There are links to Common Core: problem solving, persistence, empathy, helping others

United Kingdom: National Curriculum in England: citizenship and Personal, Social, Health and Economic education (PSHE).

New Zealand: Key Competencies of Te Whāriki: problem solving, persistence, empathy, and helping others

Follow us on twitter! @Asickmom

Copyright

ISBN 978-0-9941297-9-6

Also available as an eBook
ISBN 978-0-9941297-1-0

Published by Books for Caring Kids.
First Edition 2014, Second edition 2015
Registered with the U.S copyright office
Text and images copyright of ©Simone Colwill. (2014)

For libray cataloguing please see the last page.

Other titles available from this author

U.S English version	Spanish Version
with links to the common core.	Paperback ISBN 978-0-9941297-2-7
Recommended by teachers and doctors	eBook ISBN 978-0-9941297-3-4
Paperback ISBN 978-0-9941127-0-5	
2nd edition ISBN 978-0-9941297-8-9	
eBook ISBN 978-0-9941297-0-3	
Kindle ISBN 978-0-9941127-7-4	

All rights reserved. No part of this book may be reproduced, copied, scanned, stored in a retrieval system, recorded or transmitted in any form without prior permission in writing from the publisher, except by a reviewer who may quote brief passages in review.

My name is Jonathan. This is my sidekick, Bear. Together, we are superheroes.

Actually, we've been superheroes

...forever!

We superheroes wear cool clothes,

carry cool gadgets,

and we save the world!

And that's *cool!*

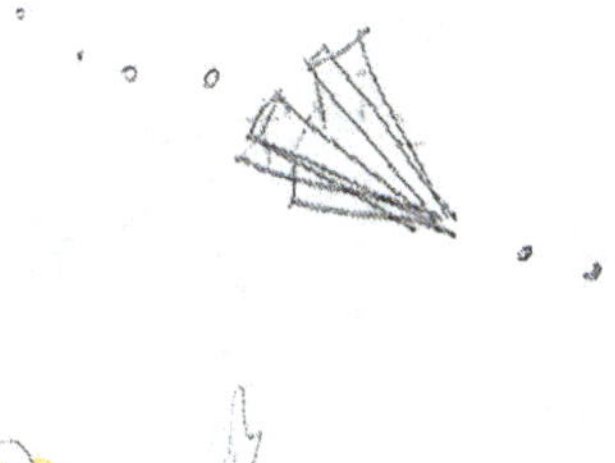

What's this? Mum is sick?

Come on Bear,
we have a new mission.

Superheroes can do *anything!*

How can I help?

"I can help," says the doctor.
"I'll find out what is wrong with your mum."

I've got just the thing! I say, giving him my magnifying glass.

We can find anything!

"I can help," says the radiographer.
"I'll take the X-ray pictures so we can see inside your mum."

These work well! I say, giving her my night-vision binoculars.

We can see anything!

"I can help," says the laboratory assistant, looking up from his microscope. "I'll catch any bugs."

These will help! I say, giving him my bug catcher and specimen jar.

We can catch anything!

"I can help," says the dietitian.
"I'll give your mum good food to make her strong."

These are yummy! I say, giving her my Choccy Bugs muesli bars.

Mummy eats these more than anything!

"I can help," says the nurse.
"I'll keep any bugs away by safely changing her dressings."

15

These are cool! I say, giving her
my bug-proof plaster bandages.

Mum will be as safe as anything!

"I can help," says the cleaner.
"I'll keep the ward clean."

These will help! I say, giving her my bug repellent.

They smell as clean as anything!

I offered to help, but no-one would listen.
Why won't anyone let me help Mum?

Maybe I should do something different?

Should I help her to run away?

Put an invisible shield around her?

Fix booster rockets to the lift?

Turbocharge the bed?

"But Super Jonny," says Mum. "You *are* helping!"

How?

"I gave the doctor your magnifying glass because he broke his glasses."

"I gave the X-ray technician your binoculars because she needed to find the next patient."

"I gave the laboratory assistant your bug catcher because he needed to store his test tubes."

"I gave the dietitian your muesli bars because she forgot her lunch."

"I gave the nurse your plasters because she cut her finger."

"And I gave the cleaner your bug repellent because she needed air freshener!"

"So you see," says Mum.
"We all used your gadgets. *They helped everybody.*"

"Wow that's *cool!*"

"You helped Mummy too!"

"Really? How?"

"By giving me lots of Superhero hugs!
And they have the power to make me
FEEEEL GOOOD!"

"My hugs have power? Really?"

"That's right," says Mum.
"The *superhero power* to make me feel good!

And that's *my* kind of medicine."

A question page for teachers and families.
Recommended by teachers as suitable for ages 3-9 years*

Thinking critically (discussion questions).

What do you think this book could be about? Look at the title and discuss.

What do you know about visiting a sick person in hospital?

What do you know about superheroes?

Contextual questions

What does a Dietitian do?
Ensures patients eat the right food to get well again.

What does a Radiographer do?
Takes the X-rays to help the doctor determine (diagnose) what is wrong.

What do Nurses do?
Nurses have many roles including: Monitoring a patient's blood pressure, pulse and temperature. They also help the patient to shower, change their clothing, sheets, and dressings—if needed.

Life skills: problem solving, persistence and empathy

What problem is Super Jonny trying to solve?
His mum is sick. He is trying to help.

How does Super Jonny try and solve this problem?
He thinks that his mum may have a bug. So he takes his gadgets to the hospital because he knows they can be used to find (p8), observe (p10), catch (p12), feed (p14), keep out (p16), and repel bugs (p18).

Super Jonny keeps offering to help, but is turned down. What does he learn?
Perseverance – keep trying until you find the answer. (There may be more than one answer.)

What motivates Jonny?
He loves his mum and feels empathy towards her.

Thinking about helping others

How do you think a person in hospital might be feeling? How could you help?

- **Frustrated and/or in pain**
- Offer to do small tasks, like put flowers into water, or help them put their slippers on.
- **Bored**
- Offer to buy them a newspaper or a magazine
- Offer to find a wheelchair and take them for a walk.
- Visit regularly, (sometimes people spend a long time in hospital).
- **Worried about home**
- Offer to feed their cat or dog at home (if they have one).
- Offer to collect their mail.

Processing information (including **oral**, **written**, and **visual** language)

Read or look for other books about hospitals.

Where did the author get the idea for this story? It is based on a true story (see writer's bio).

Retell the story using a different character in the book.

Explain the message of the story.

Share information with the class.

*because of subject matter

Preparing for a hospital admission

5 tips for chronically ill mums.

If you know there is a chance you will be admitted, here are a few pointers to help. Don't worry, if you don't get them done, as you can show this list to another adult who can help.

Consider...

1. Putting a couple of packets of your child's favourite biscuits in your hospital bag. Kids are always hungry and are delighted to see you have not forgotten them!

2. Pack a couple of easy-to-read kids' books. (Don't worry if you're not up to reading to them, if they can read, let them read to you!). They can still snuggle up on the bed beside you, BUT, make sure they are on the opposite side of the IV stand. (Your nurse can help you).

3. Hospitals nearly always have vending machines. Pack some loose change and let your child make a selection. This is fun and can include a little math activity, by getting them to count out the change.

4. Download a new movie onto your electronic device, and only let the kids watch it when they come to visit. Or, take a DVD into the hospital as there is often a DVD player on the ward.

5. Pack some toys. A pack of cards, some travel games, or a colouring-in book can be really handy. Often, there are other children around who are looking for something to do too!

...For more tips, please sign up for my newsletter,

www.sickmom.org

Other titles available from this author

U.S English version
with links to the common core.
Recommended by teachers and doctors
Paperback   ISBN 978-0-9941127-0-5
2nd edition ISBN 978-0-9941297-8-9
eBook   ISBN 978-0-9941297-0-3
Kindle   ISBN 978-0-9941127-7-4

Spanish Version
Paperback ISBN 978-0-9941297-2-7
eBook   ISBN 978-0-9941297-3-4

Simone Colwill

Simone trained as a radiation therapist at Auckland hospital. She is married to Nick, and they live with their family in Auckland, New Zealand. She has Crohn's disease. This is Simone's first book for kids, and is based on a true story.

Jasmine Ting

Jasmine is a graphic designer and illustrator. This is her first venture into children's illustration. You can find Jasmine's work online at www.Behance.net and various social platforms.

If you enjoyed this book, please help the author by leaving a good review on amazon. For more books by this author, please see www.sickmom.org

Library catalguing: 1. Cancer, juvenile fiction. 2. Diabetes, juvenile fiction. 3 Heart disease, juvenile fiction. 4. Hospitals, picture books. 5 Sick parents, picture books. 6. Helpful behaviour, picture books. 7. Chronic illness, juvenile fiction.

www.ingramcontent.com/pod-product-compliance
Lightning Source LLC
Chambersburg PA
CBHW080519020526
44113CB00055B/2536